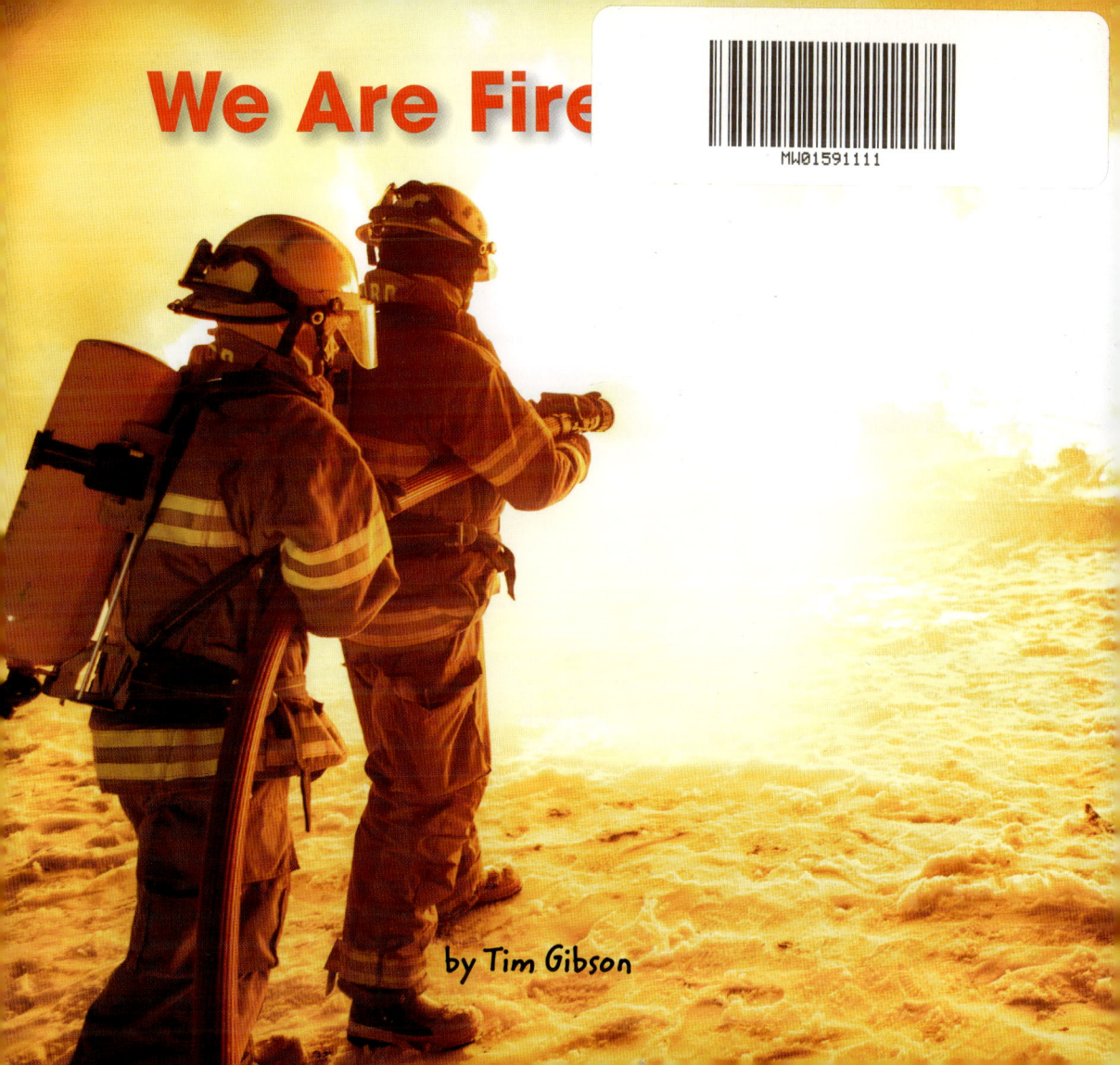

We Are Fire

by Tim Gibson

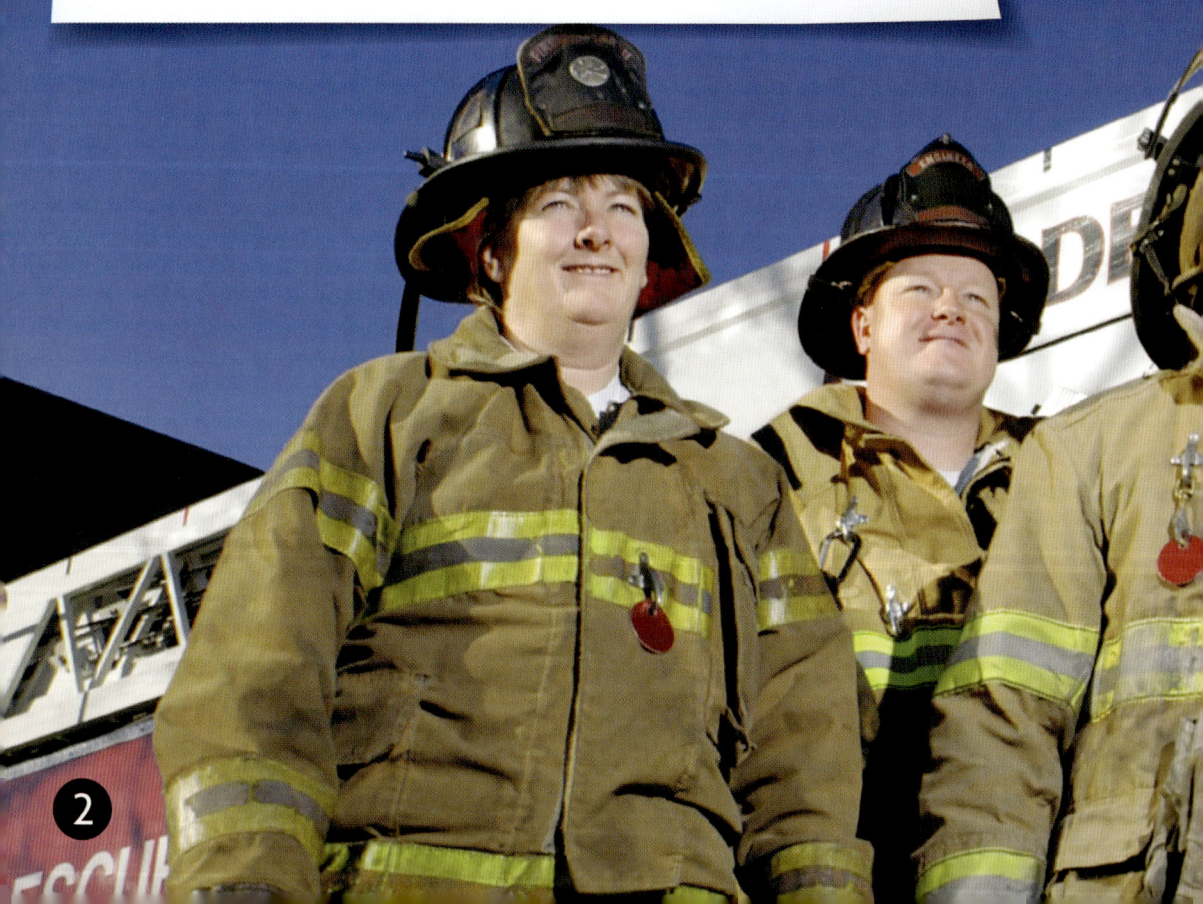

We are firefighters.

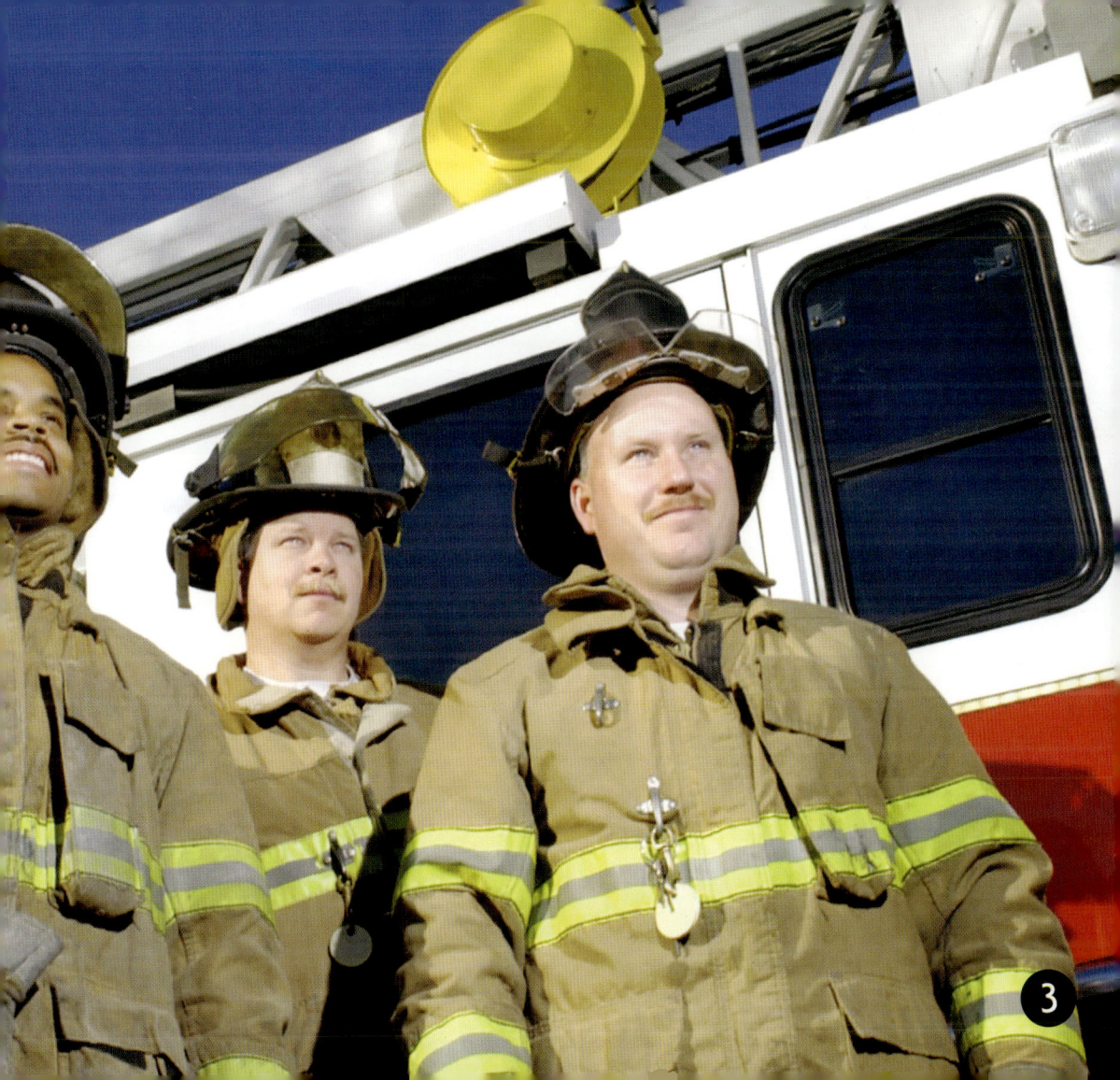

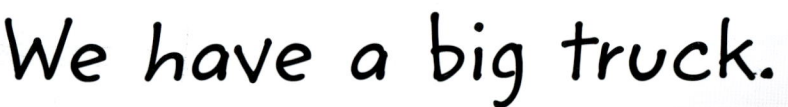

We have a big truck.

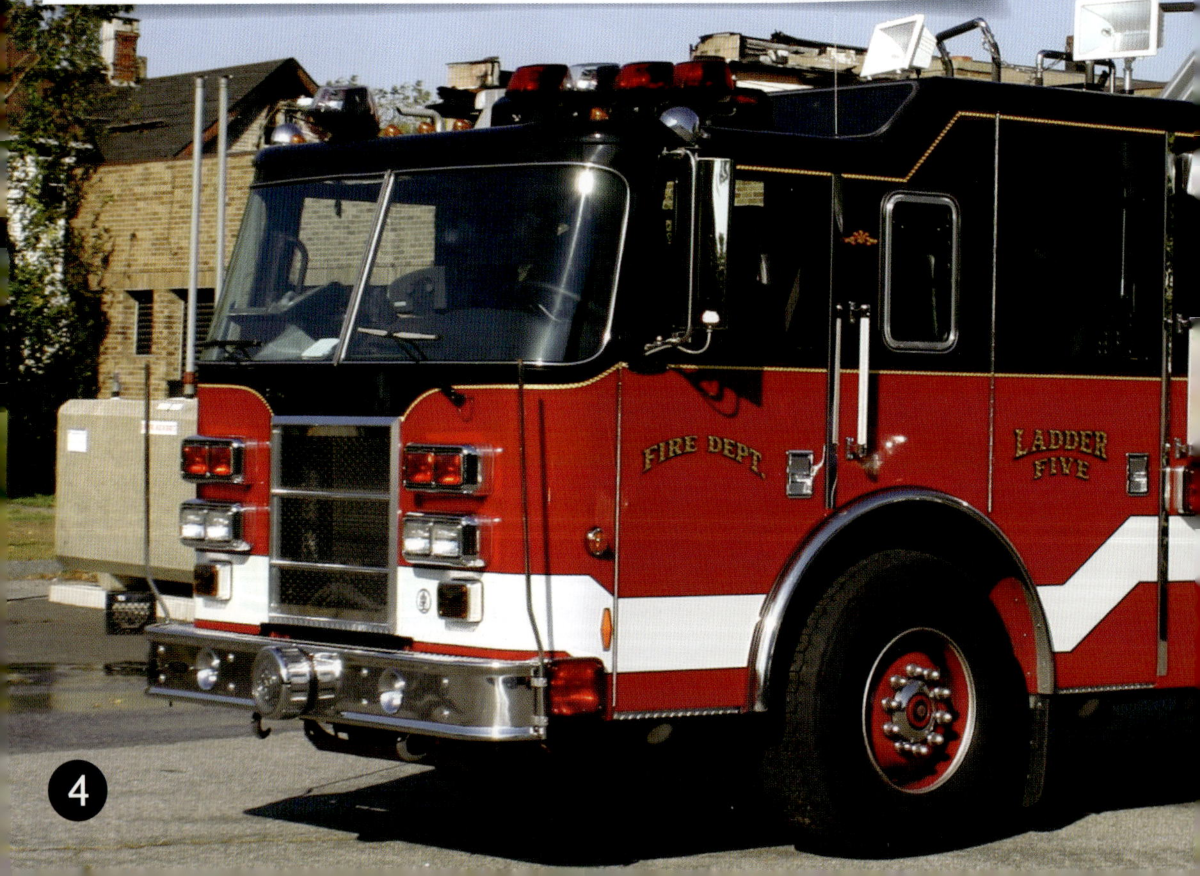

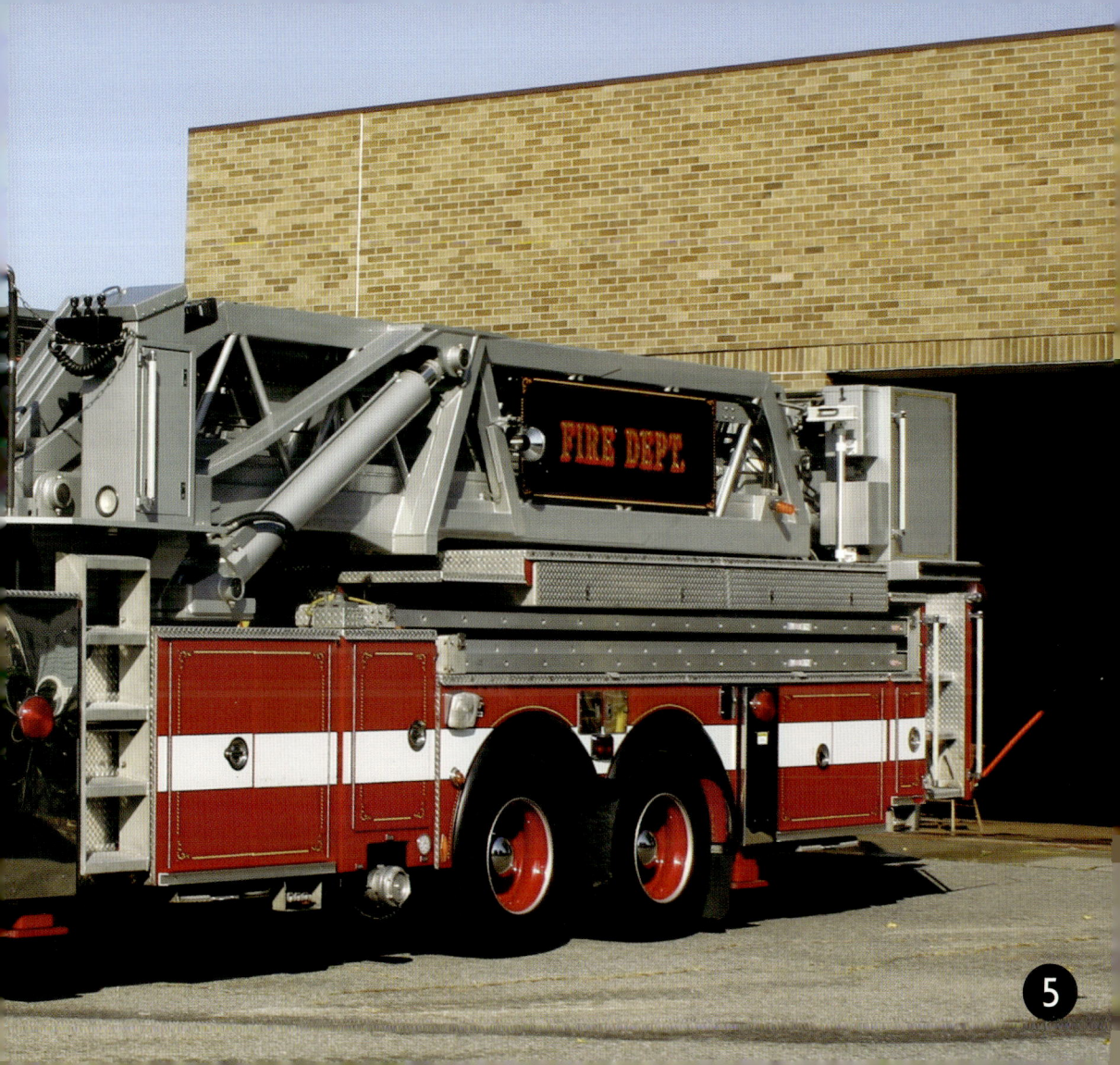

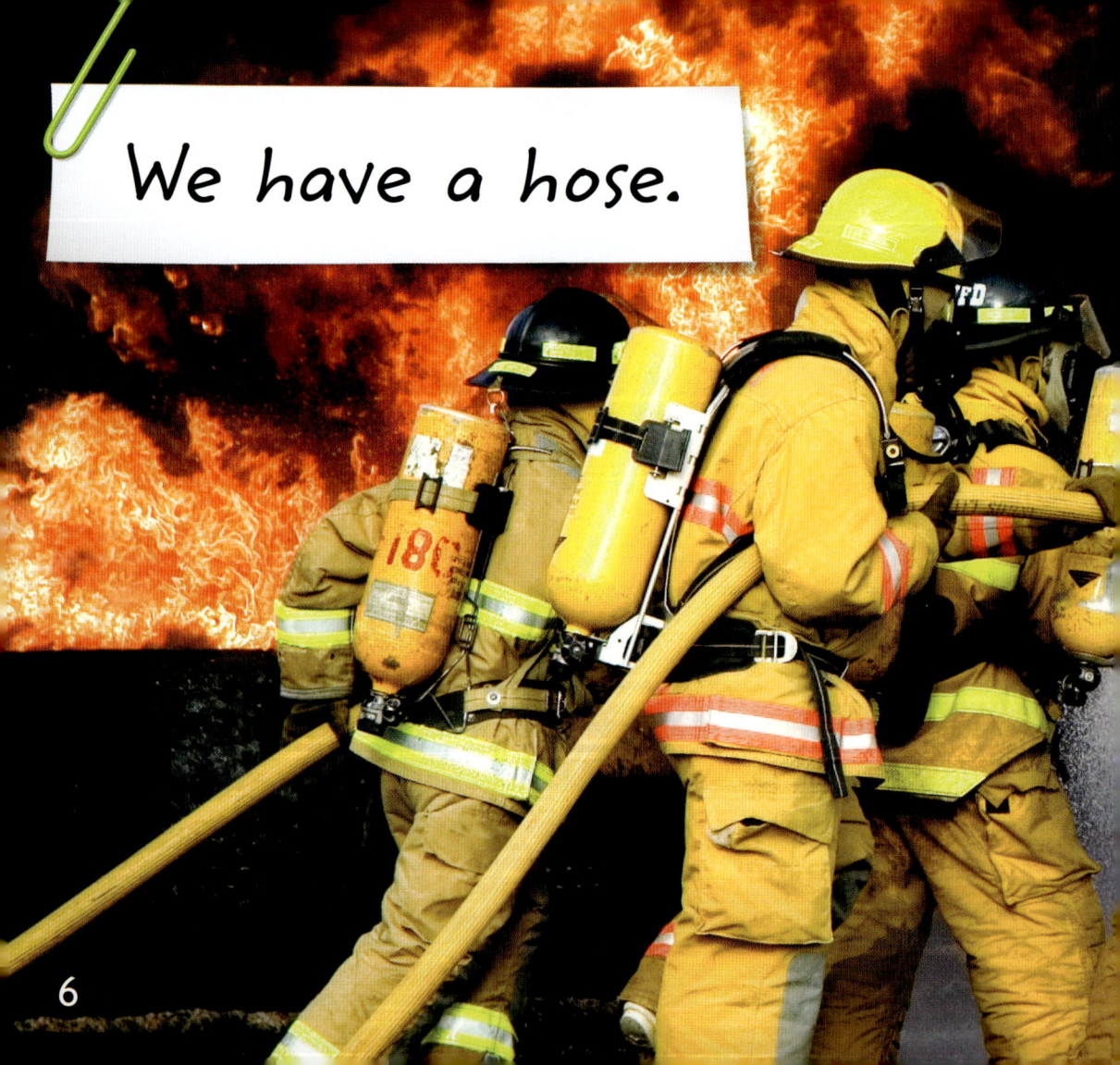

We have a hose.

6

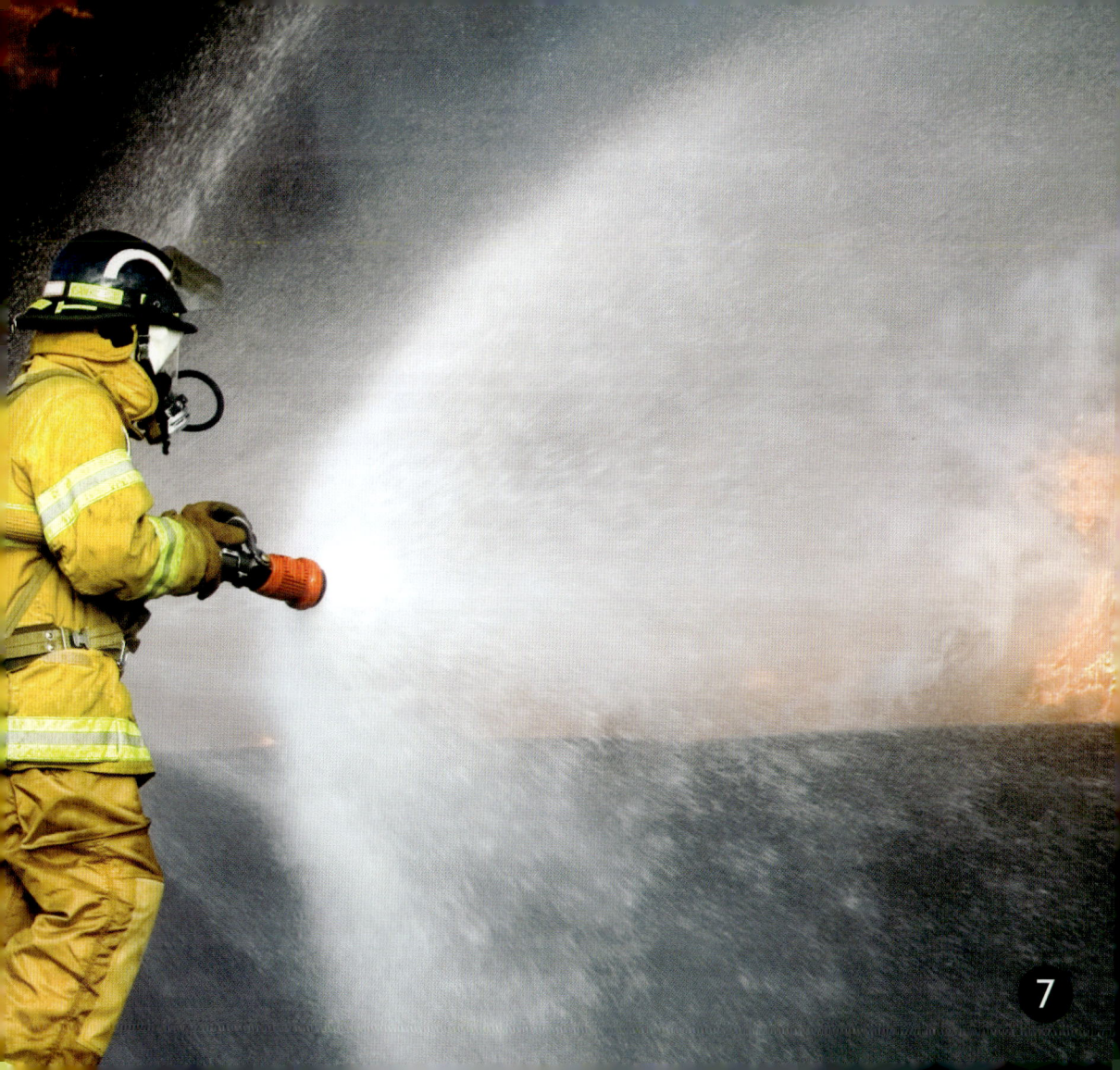

We help people.
We help cats and dogs.

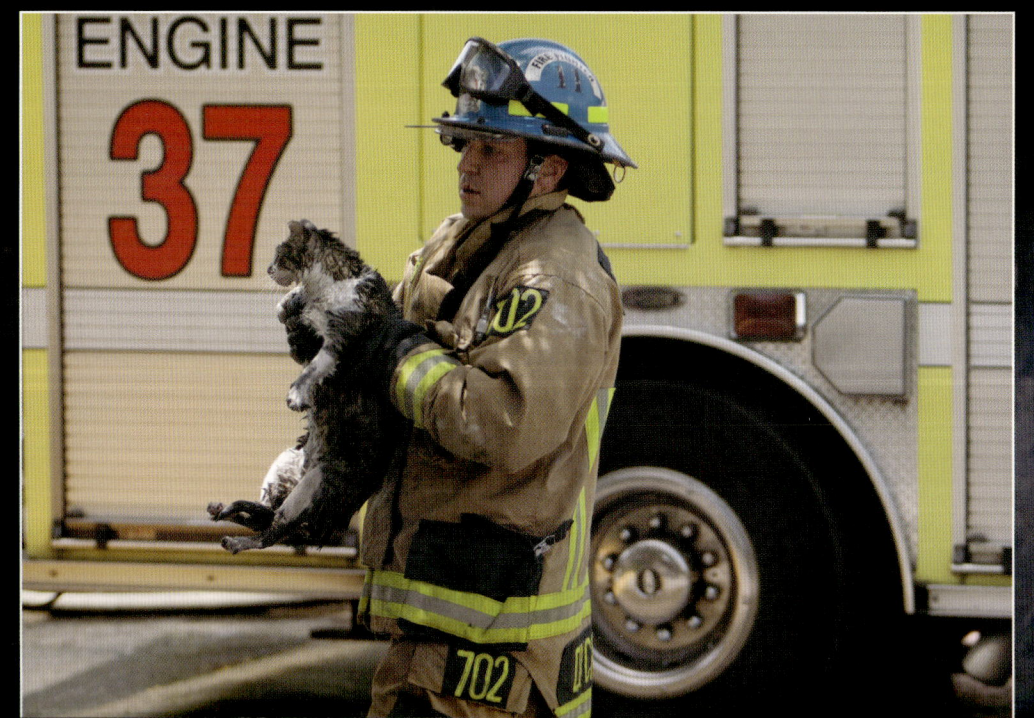

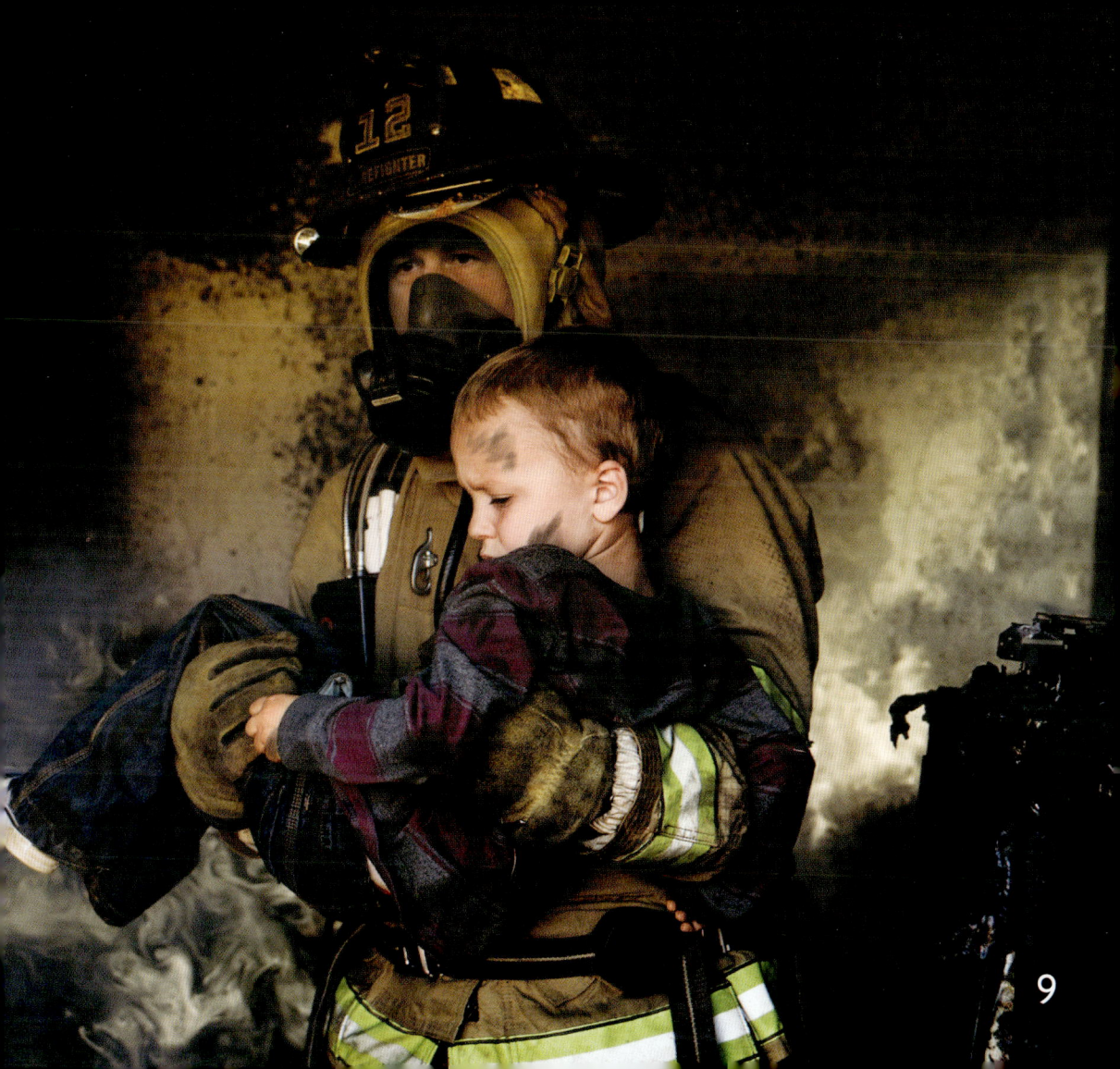

We help make homes safe.

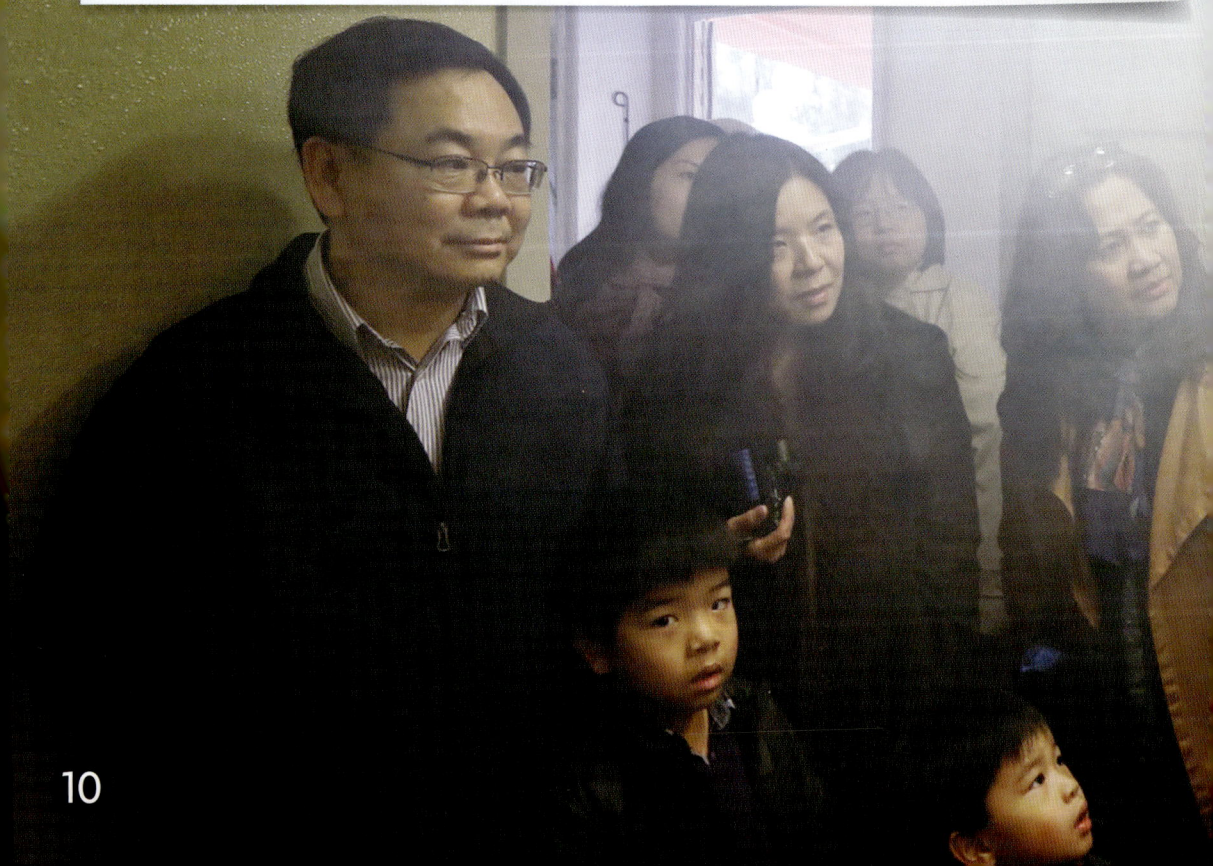

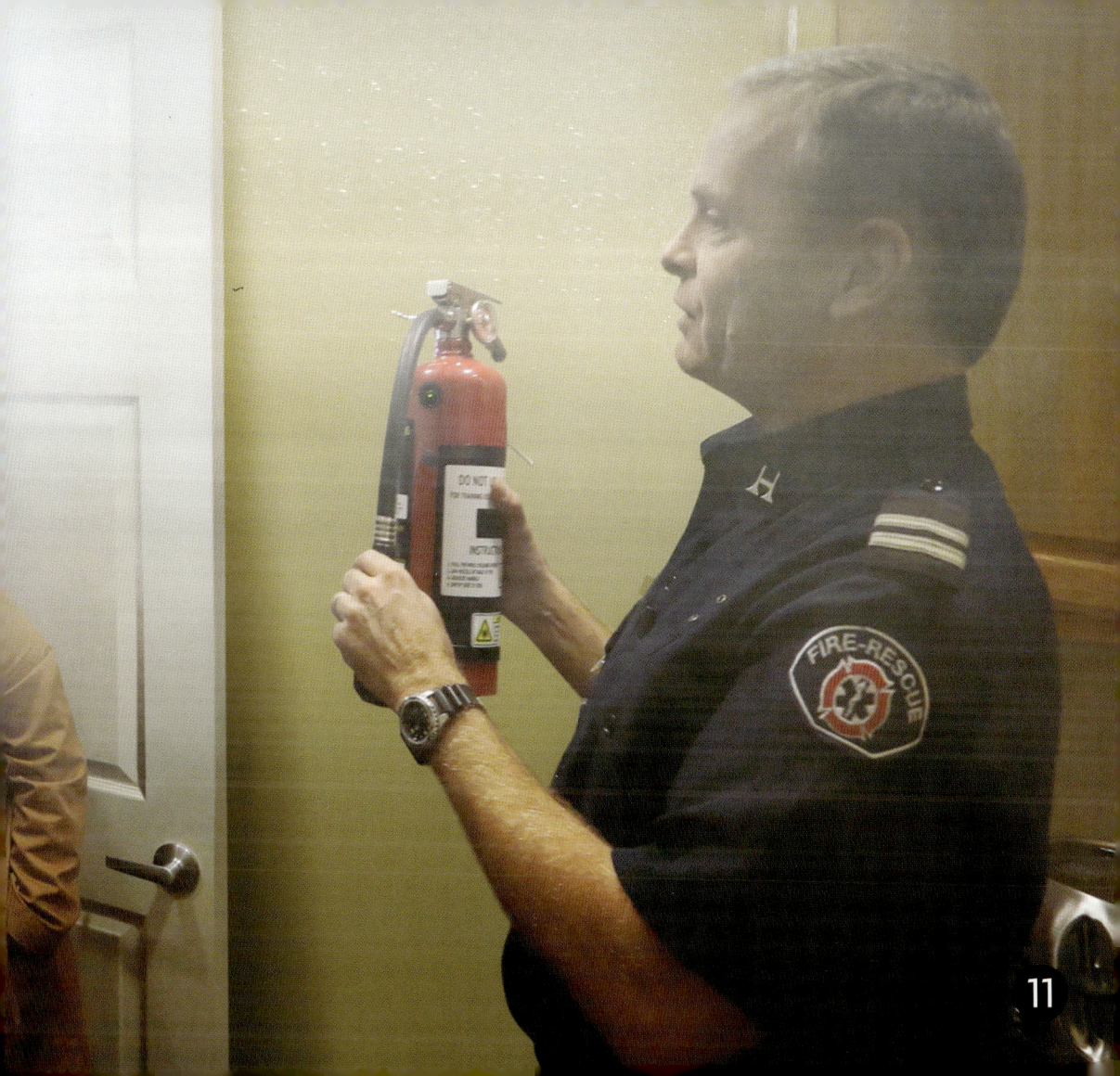

We help make people safe.

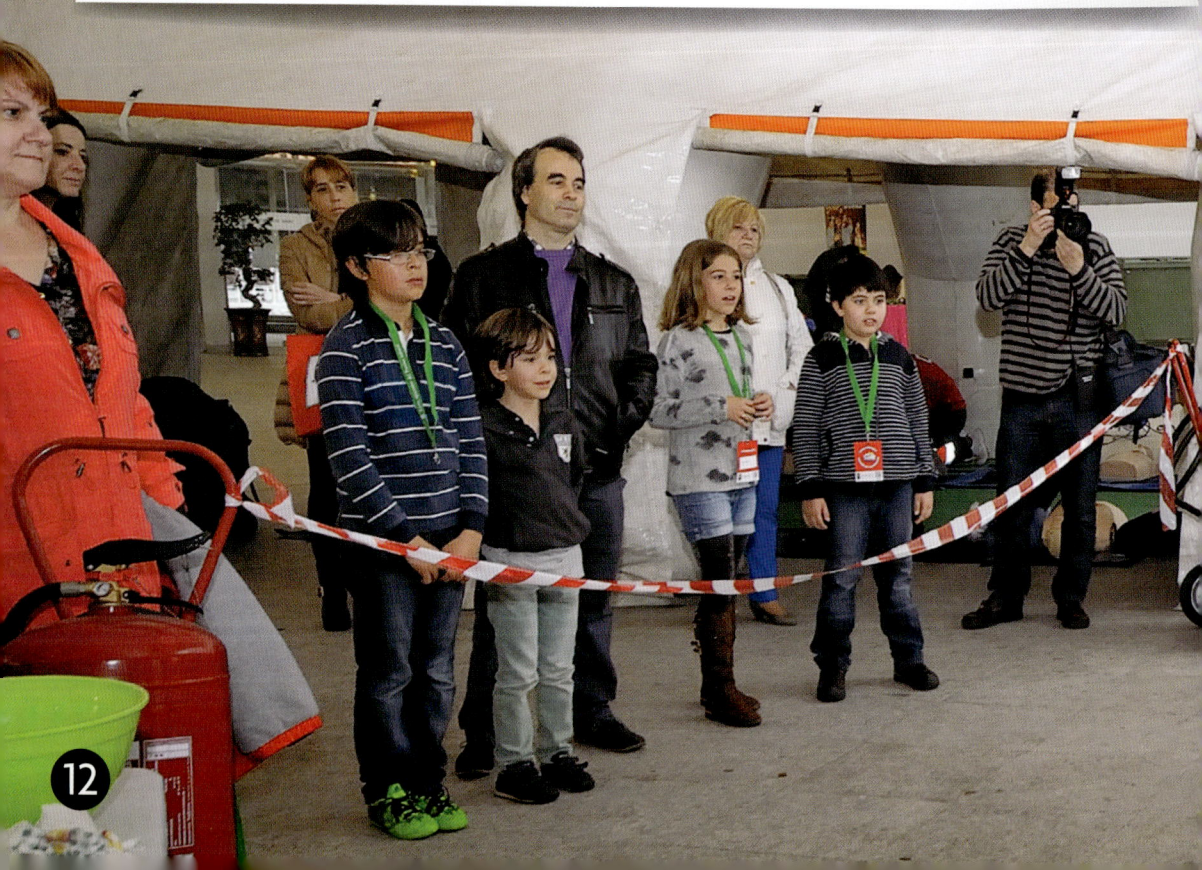

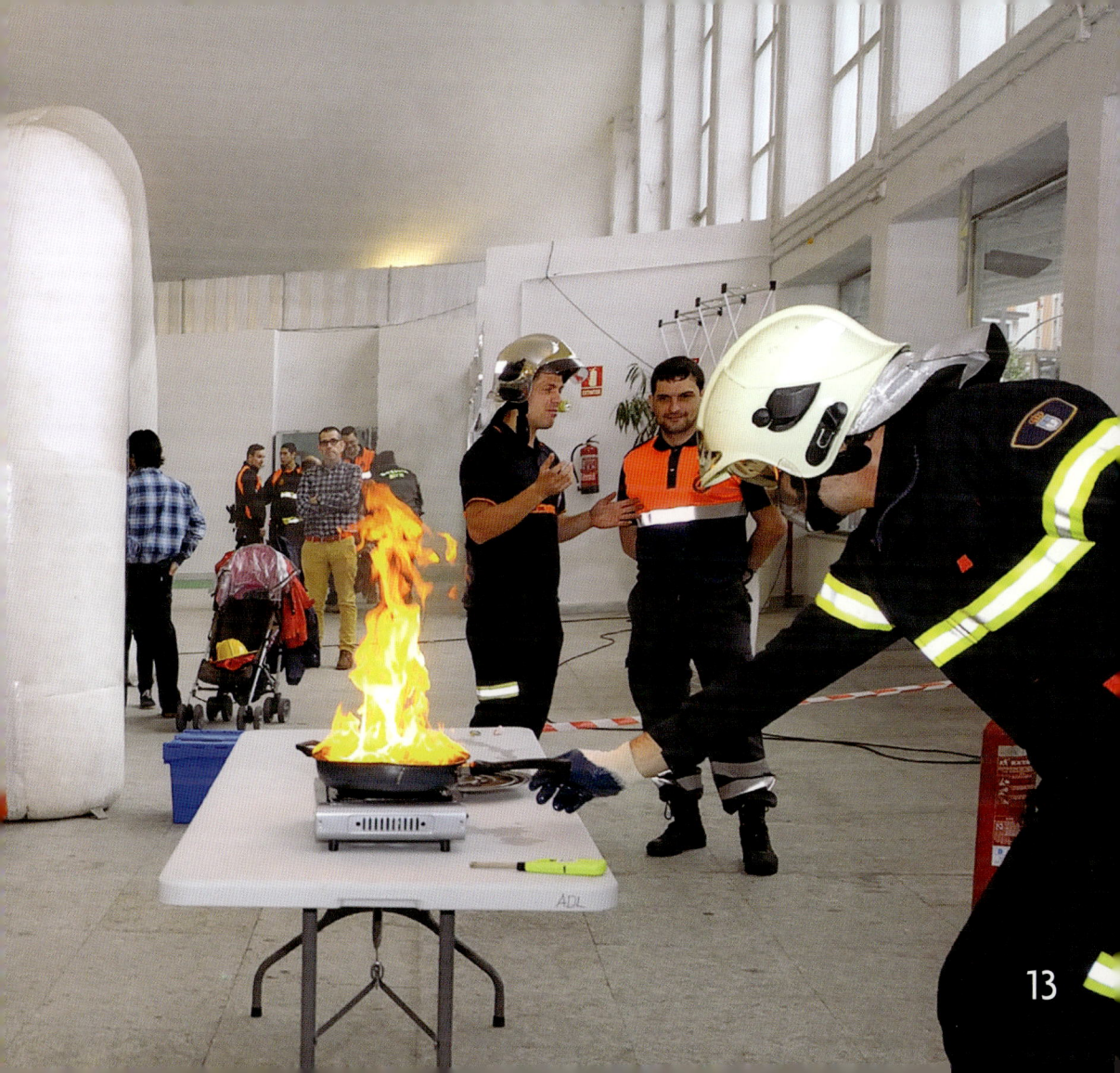

13

We clean the firehouse.

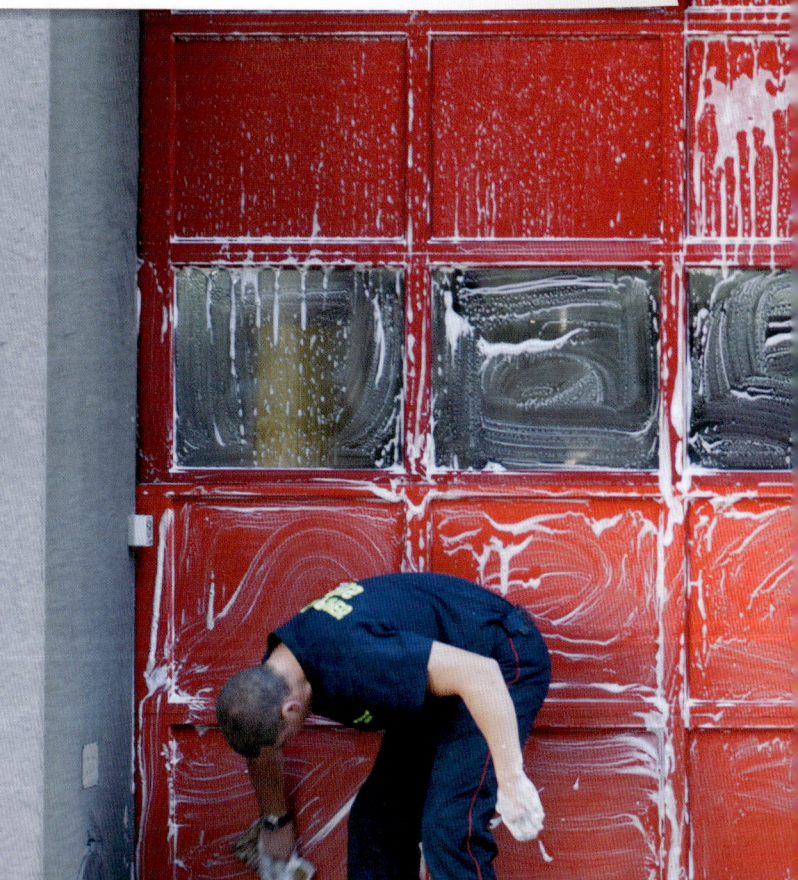

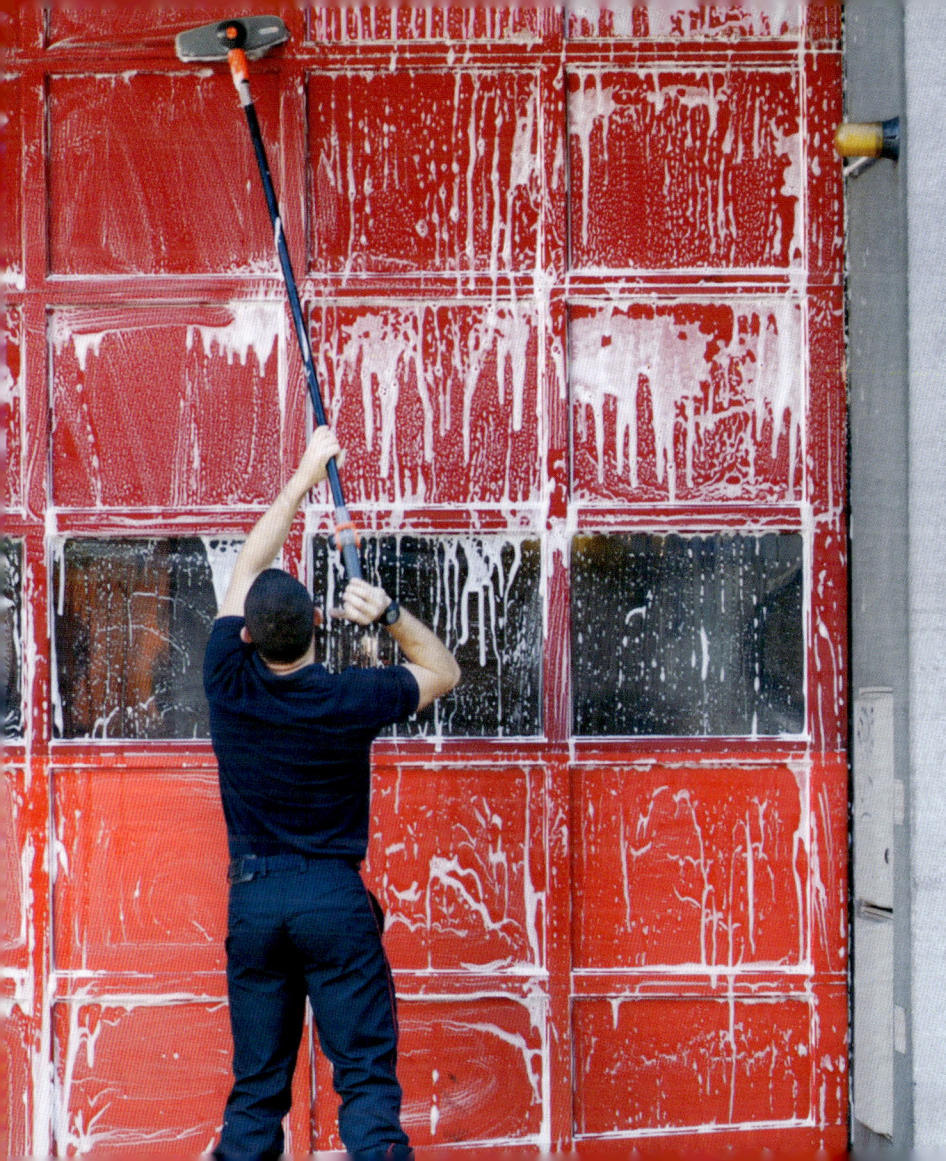

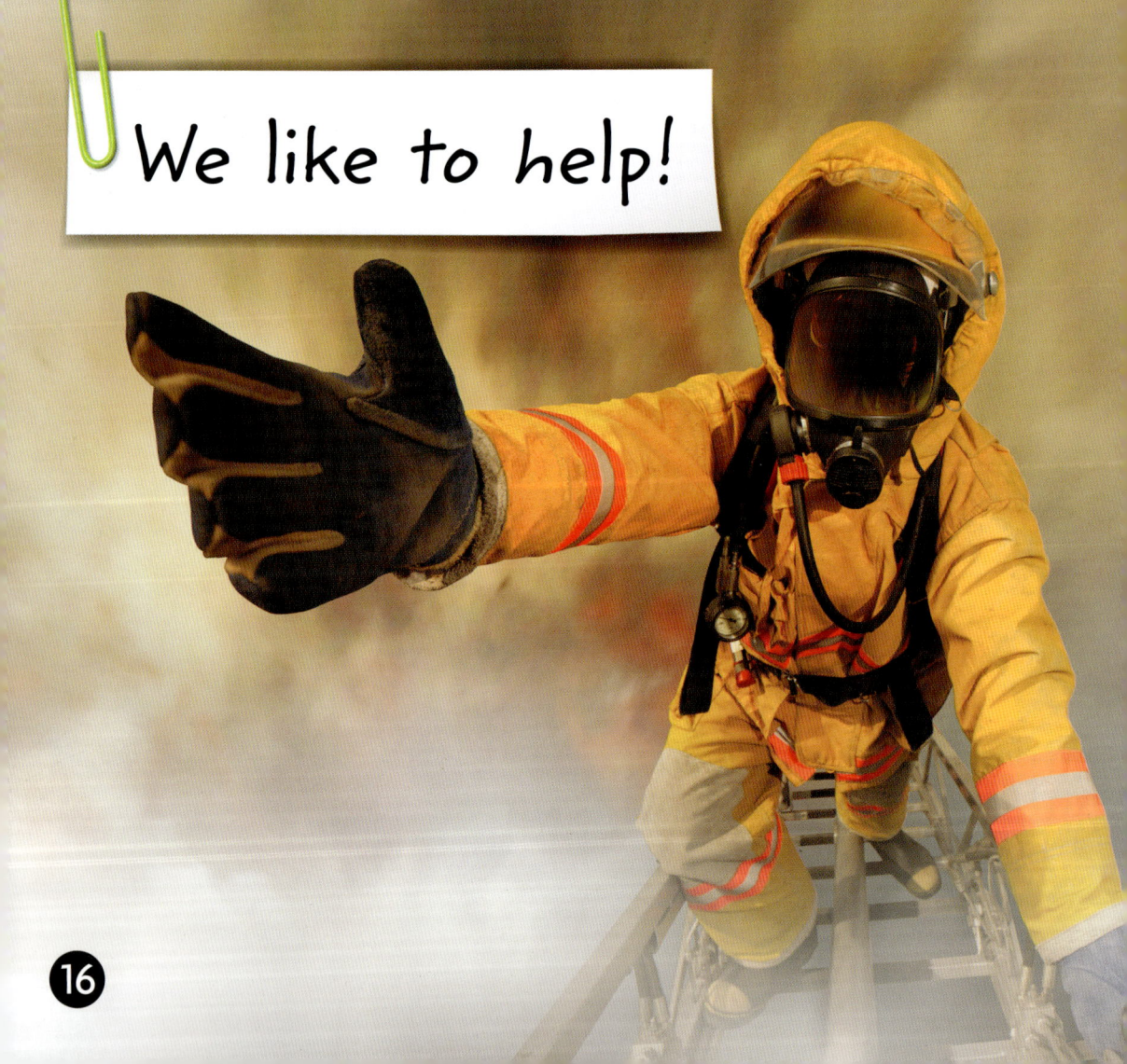

We like to help!